LET'S LOOK AT
Bugs

Nicola Tuxworth

LORENZ BOOKS
NEW YORK • LONDON • SYDNEY • BATH

Beetles

Beetles can be different shapes, sizes and colors.

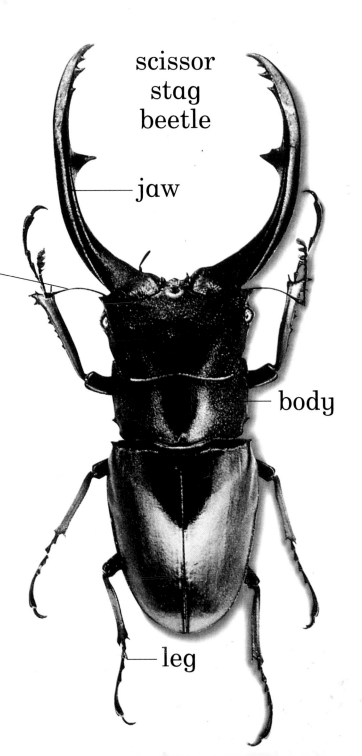

scissor stag beetle

jaw

antenna

body

leg

tropical tortoise beetle

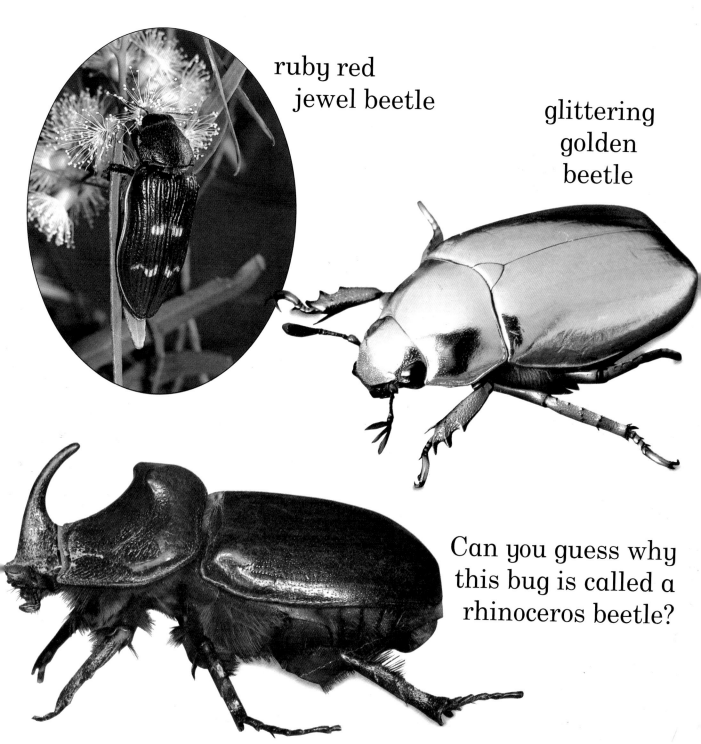

ruby red
jewel beetle

glittering
golden
beetle

Can you guess why
this bug is called a
rhinoceros beetle?

Ladybirds

A ladybird is a small, spotty beetle.

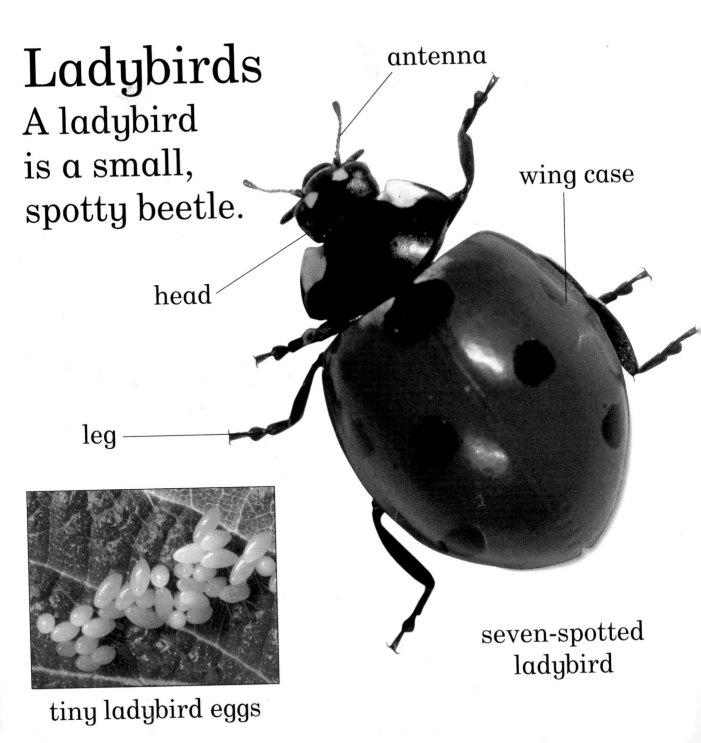

antenna

wing case

head

leg

tiny ladybird eggs

seven-spotted ladybird

A ladybird has tough, spotty wing cases.

Ladybirds hide away all through the winter.

What color is this ladybird?

Bumble-bees

A bumble-bee
has a striped,
furry body and
a loud buzz.

leg

bumble-bee

wing

A bumble-bee
flies from
flower...

... to flower.

Honey-bees

A honey-bee
makes sweet,
sticky honey.

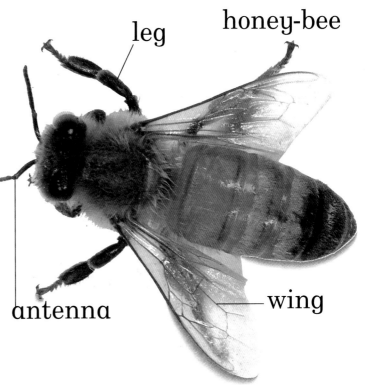

honey-bee

leg

antenna

wing

Honey-bees live
together in a hive ...

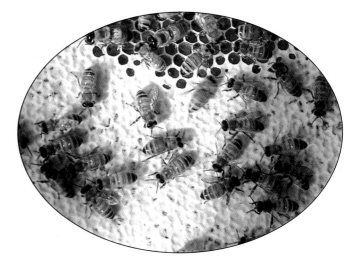

... and make honey!

Locusts

Locusts live in hot, dry places.

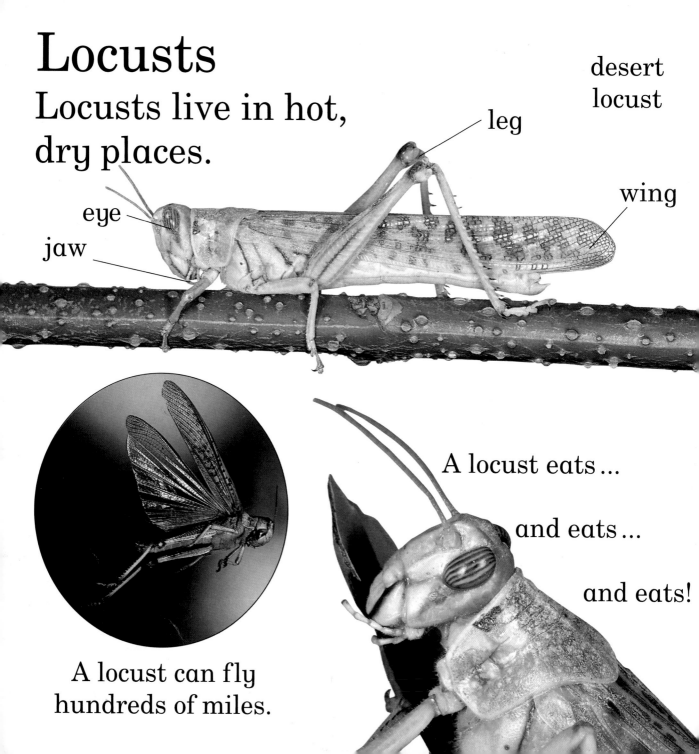

desert locust

leg

wing

eye

jaw

A locust eats ...

and eats ...

and eats!

A locust can fly hundreds of miles.

Grasshoppers

A grasshopper lives in fields and meadows.

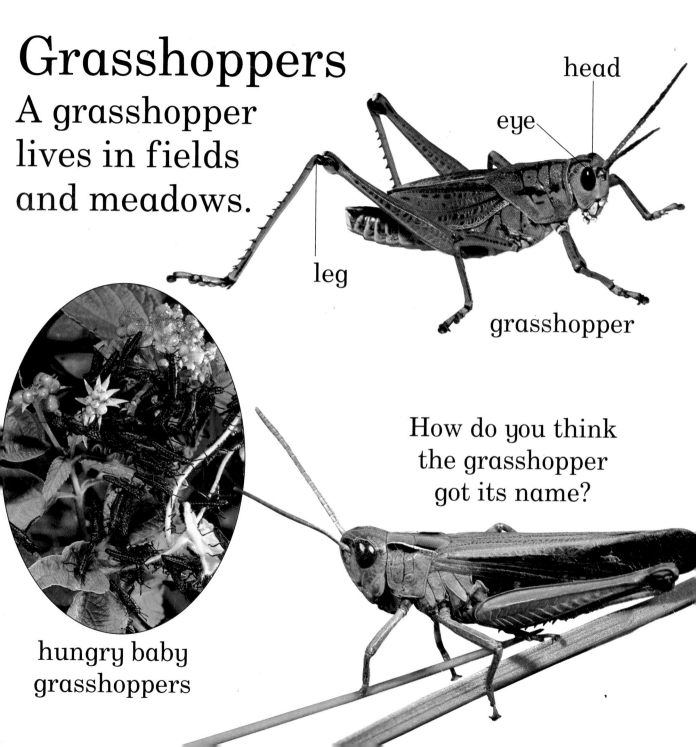

head

eye

leg

grasshopper

How do you think the grasshopper got its name?

hungry baby grasshoppers

Moths

Most moths rest
during the day,
and fly about
at night.

body

antenna

front wing

Emperor
moth

back wing

From a tiny egg ... ... hatches a hungry caterpillar

How many spots
can you see?

...that changes into a pupa.

When the
pupa splits
open, a moth
crawls out!

Butterfly

A butterfly's wings are covered in tiny scales.

eye

Swallowtail butterfly

back wing

front wing

This hairy caterpillar will turn into...

...a beautiful butterfly!

How many butterflies
can you count
on this flower?

stripey zebra
butterfly

The spots on
this butterfly
look like eyes!

Ants

Busy ants live
together in
large groups.

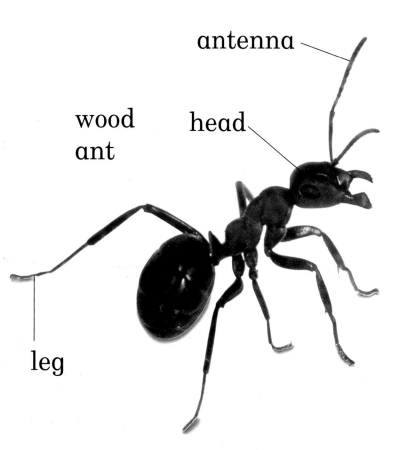

antenna

wood
ant

head

leg

black winged ants

tiny ant
eggs

marching
ants

Why do you think
these ants are called
leafcutter ants?

Wasps

Wasps have brightly colored bodies and a painful sting.

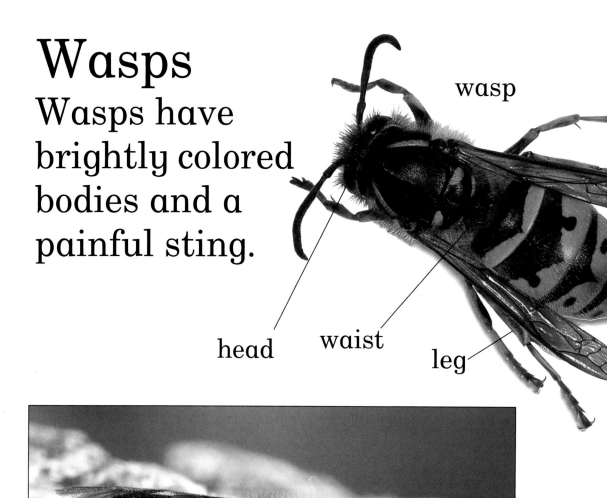

wasp

head

waist

leg

shiny, ruby-tail wasp

What can you
see inside the
papery nest?

Wasps have
strong legs ...

...and very
powerful
jaws!

Flies

A fly has one pair of wings and six padded feet.

foot

eye

fly

leg

wing

A fly can walk upside down...

...and taste food through its feet!

Dragonflies

A dragonfly
zooms around
near ponds
and streams.

front wing

back wing

body

darter
dragonfly

leg

dazzling, darting dragonfly

Look at these
huge eyes!

Which bug is which?

Can you remember the names of all these different bugs?